VERN McLELLAN

HARVEST HOUSE PUBLISHERS
Eugene, Oregon 97402

CREAM OF WIT

Copyright © 1991 by Vern McLellan
Published by Harvest House Publishers
Eugene, Oregon 97402

Library of Congress Cataloging-in-Publication Data

McLellan, Vernon K.
    Cream of wit / by Vern McLellan.
    ISBN 0-89081-859-2
    1. Conduct of life—Humor.   I. Title
PN6162.M347   1991   90-23652
    081—dc20   CIP

To my grandchildren—
Jon, Julie, Jaclyn, and Emmalee
—the cream of the crop

Contents

Introduction

As you face life's daily m-ooo-sic, I hope you'll milk *Cream of Wit* for all it's worth!

What fun whipping up these creamy quotes and anecdotes!

It's amazing where you can spot these quips, quotes, and witticisms! As I've strolled down the cowpath of life, I've discovered them on the side of a truck, in a local farm journal, in a church bulletin, on a billboard, on a place mat, in a noncopyrighted publication, on an office noteboard....

I have tried to give credit to authors and sources—but so often a one-liner or short story appears without a label. If you know the source of an unidentified statement in *Cream of Wit*, please let me know so credit can be given.

I read a billboard slogan recently: "Milk—it does your body good!" The milk of truth does your mind and spirit good! The apostle Peter put it this way: "Desire the pure milk of the word, that you may grow thereby..." (1 Peter 2:2 NKJV).

I trust you'll be inspired, encouraged, and challenged by these oft-humorous but thought-provoking proverbs and principles.

————

Holding a drippy ice cream cone precariously, five-year-old Janie stepped into the elevator with her mother. A fashionably dressed lady gasped, stiffened, gathered her expensive fur coat around her, and retreated to the corner of the elevator.

"Watch out, Janie," the mother exclaimed. "Be careful you don't get any hairs in your ice cream!"

When all is said or done, life is simply how you view it!

M-ooo-ving right along, I think I'll apply some vanishing cream and disappear through the barn door some city slicker left open!

—Vern McLellan
Charlotte, North Carolina

Laughing Stock

The cow: God's jolly cafeteria with four legs and a tail—*E.M. Root.*

―――――――

Hey diddle diddle,
The cat and the fiddle
The cow jumped over the moon;
The little dog laughed
To see such sport,
And the dish ran away with the spoon.

―――――――

The reason the cow jumped over the moon was because there was a short circuit in the milking machine.

―――――――

The cow knows not what her tail is worth till she has lost it—*George Herbert.*

Nature is amazing; who would have thought of growing a fly swatter on the rear end of a cow?

———————

A Quaker's cow switched him with her tail, then stepped into the bucket, then kicked the milk bucket over.

"Cow, thou knowest that I love thee and that I would not harm thee. Thou knowest that thou aggravatest me with thy tail. Thou knowest that I would say naught when thou steppeth into the bucket, but what thou did not knowest when thou kickest the bucket over is that I'm going to sell thee to a Methodist and I hope he kicks the living daylights out of thee."

———————

The little city boy stood and watched the farmer milk the only cow he had. The next morning the farmer was much excited, as the cow had been stolen during the night.

Farmer: Drat the thief that stole that cow. He's miles away from here by now.

Little boy: I wouldn't worry 'bout it, mister; they can't get so far away with it, 'cause you drained her crankcase last night.

They strolled down the lane together,
   The sky was studded with stars.
They reached the gate in silence,
   And he lifted up the bars.
She neither smiled or thanked him,
   For indeed she knew not how.
For he was just a farmer boy,
   And she—a Jersey cow.

———

Elsie: Say, Eldon, how did you get that swelling on your nose?

Eldon: I bent down to smell a brose.

Elsie: Not "brose"—"rose." There's no *b* in rose.

Eldon: Yeah? Well, there was one in this one!

———

The cow is of the bovine ilk;
One end is moo, the other milk.
          —Ogden Nash

———

Boy: Ah, look at the cow and the calf rubbing noses in the pasture. That sight makes me want to do the same.

Girl: Well, go ahead—it's your cow.

This sign was attached to the gate of a pasture evidently used as a lovers' lane: Please close the gate. The heifer you're chasing is easier to catch than mine.

Argue

You can argue with her "till the cows come home," but she'll never change her mind.

———

My mind's made up—don't confuse me with the facts!

———

To avoid a hot argument, keep a cool head.

———

An argument: Two people trying to get the last word in first.

———

When arguing with a fool, be sure he isn't doing the same thing.

———

There are always two sides to an argument—but no end.

Even a woman finds it difficult to argue with a man who won't talk.

Choice

You cannot sell the cow and drink the milk. (It's one or the other—you can't have both.)

———

You can't have your cake and eat it too.

———

The choice is simple—you can either stand up and be counted, or lie down and be counted out.

———

Sign on a businessman's desk: My decision is maybe—and that's final.

———

Which will it be for you? Jawbone, wishbone, or backbone?

———

Always take plenty of time to make a snap decision.

Prayer: Let the words of my mouth, and the meditation of my heart, be acceptable in thy sight, O Lord, my strength, and my redeemer (Psalm 19:14 KJV).

Determination

It doesn't matter how you feel, the cows have to be milked—*Bill Andreas*, Ohio state basketballer on why he played in a game while injured.

If at first you don't succeed—you're running about average!

No one knew this better than Thomas Edison, who, to find a substitute for lead in the manufacture of storage batteries, conducted 20,000 unsuccessful experiments.

A reporter asked him: "Aren't you discouraged by all this waste of effort?"

"Waste?" he shot back. "Nothing is wasted. I've found 20,000 things that don't work."

We can go through life obsessed by failure, and refuse to pick ourselves up and try again. Or we can learn from past mistakes to devise new approaches.

Most of this world's useful work is done by people who are pressed for time, stretched to the limit, or don't feel well.

———

No pain—no gain!

Down in the Bottle

Some men battle their way to the top then bottle their way to the bottom.

———

A hangover is the moaning after the night before.

———

A hangover is something to occupy the head that wasn't used the night before.

———

A drinking man commits suicide on the installment plan.

———

Stop and think before you drink. Boozers are losers.

The horse and mule live thirty years,
   And nothing know of wines and beers.
The goats and sheep at twenty die,
   And never taste of Scotch and Rye.

The cow drinks water by the ton,
   And at eighteen is mostly done.
The dog at fifteen cashes in
   Without the aid of rum and gin.

The cat in milk and water soaks
   And then in twelve short years it croaks.
The modest, sober, bone-dry hen
   Lays eggs for nogs, then dies at ten.

All animals are strictly dry,
   They sinless live and swiftly die.
But sinful, ginful rum-soaked men
   Survive for threescore years and ten.
And some of them, a very few,
   Stay pickled 'til they're ninety-two.

Wine gives false courage; hard liquor leads to brawls; what fools men are to let it master them, making them reel drunkenly down the street! (Proverbs 20:1).

Traffic warning sign: Heads you win—cocktails you lose!

Gossip

The gossiping sort have a cow's tongue—a smooth side and a rough side—*William Ellis*.

————————

A gossip is just a fool with a keen sense of rumor

————————

People who gossip usually wind up in their own mouth traps.

————————

A gossip is a person who jumps to conclusions, takes people at deface value, and knows how to add to and to.

————————

There's so much good in the worst of us, and so much bad in the best of us, that it's hardly appropriate for any of us to talk about the rest of us

————————

An evil man sows strife; gossip separates the best of friends (Proverbs 16:28).

————————

Fire goes out for a lack of fuel, and tensions disappear when gossip stops (Proverbs 26:20).

Meditation

> Yet true it is, as cow chaws cud,
>   And trees at spring do yield forth bud,
> Except wind stands as never it stood,
>   It is an ill wind turns none to good.
> > —*Thomas Tusser*

A city girl visiting her uncle on the farm was watching a cow chewing her cud.

"Pretty fine cow, that," said her uncle as he came by.

"Yes," the girl, "But doesn't it cost a lot to keep her in chewing gum?"

> Fear less, hope more,
>   Eat less, chew more,
> Whine less, breathe more,
>   Talk less, say more,
> Hate less, love more,
>   And all good things will be yours.
> > —*Swedish proverb*

No great work has ever been produced except after a long interval of still and musing meditation—*Walter Bagehot*.

The gum-chewing student,
  The cud-chewing cow,
Are somewhat alike,
  Yet different somehow.
Just what is the difference
  I think I know now—
It's the thoughtful look
  On the face of the cow.

———————

Meditation is the door to wisdom.

Opinions

He told him "how the cow ate the cabbage." (He told him a thing or two about a lot of things.)

———————

Men who never retract their opinions love themselves more than they love truth.

———————

Everyone's entitled to my opinion.

———————

A fanatic is one who can't change his opinion and won't change the subject.

People generally have too many opinions and not enough convictions.

―――――――

Every person has a right to his opinion, but no one has a right to be wrong about the facts.

―――――――

An opinion is usually a prejudice with a few unrelated facts.

―――――――

You're prejudiced when you weigh the facts with your thumb on the scales.

Opportunity

Milk the cow which is near. Why pursue the one which runs away?—*Theocritus.*

―――――――

The man who hunts two rabbits will catch neither.

―――――――

The trouble with opportunities is that they are always more recognizable going than coming.

A wise youth makes hay while the sun shines, but what a shame to see a lad who sleeps away his hour of opportunity (Proverbs 10:5).

————

Make hay while the sun shines.

————

Opportunity knocks, but it has never been known to turn the knob and walk in.

————

When you have a chance to embrace an opportunity, give it a big hug.

————

Most of us don't recognize opportunity until we see it working for a competitor—*Jay Huenfeld*.

————

Opportunity knocks only once but temptation bangs on the door for years.

Procrastination

The man who procrastinates struggles with catastrophe.

Few people are fast enough to keep up with all their good intentions.

———

A procrastinator suffers from hardening of the oughteries.

———

Procrastination is my sin, it brings me naught but sorrow, I know that I should stop it, in fact, I will—tomorrow!—*Gloria Pitzer*.

———

Procrastination is the thief of time.

———

He who doesn't want to make bread sifts the flour all day.

———

Procrastination is the devil's chloroform.

Talk

She who could talk the hide off a cow could also talk a cow out of her calf.

One Arizona farmer put it this way: My wife always has the last word—and all the words before it.

———

There is now a female computer on the market. You didn't ask it anything, but it tells you anyway.

———

Only an echo keeps a woman from having the last word.

———

Keep your mouth closed and you'll stay out of trouble (Proverbs 21:23).

———

Our church was in the process of finding a new pastor. One candidate stayed for an evening service and agreed to accept questions from the congregation.

During the session, a parishioner asked if the minister was familiar with farming, since our church is in the midst of a rural community.

"No," the minister replied. "My wife was raised on a dairy farm, but I grew up on the beaches of Southern California. All I knew was surfing and swimming. I never saw a cow until I met my wife."—*Leila Weddle in* Reader's Digest.

Wife: What's the idea? You yawned seven times while I was talking to you.

Husband: No I didn't. I was trying to say something.

———

It's not polite to talk with a full mouth or an empty head.

———

The best way to save face is to keep the lower part shut.

———

When you're in deep water, be sure to keep your mouth shut.

Smile

There was an old man who said, "How
Shall I flee from this horrible cow?

I will sit on this stile, and continue to smile,
Which may soften the heart of that cow."
—*Edward Lear*

———

The curve of a smile can set a lot of things straight.

A smile is the lighting system of the face and the heating system of the heart.

———

A happy face means a glad heart; a sad face means a breaking heart (Proverbs 15:13).

———

A warm smile thaws an icy stare.

———

All people smile in the same language.

———

A smile improves your face value.

———

When you see someone without a smile, give him one of yours.

———

The businessman who does not have a smiling face should not open his shop.

———

Why not wear a smile? It's just about the only thing you can wear that isn't taxed.

To make a smile come, so they say,
   Brings thirteen muscles into play,
While if you want a frown to thrive,
   You've got to work up sixty-five.

———————

One thing is certain—smiles never go up in price or down in value.

———————

The nice thing about wearing a smile is one size fits everybody.

———————

He who wants to spoil the day for a grouch should give him a smile.

———————

Smiles is the longest word in the world. There's a mile between the first and last letters in the word.

The Cream Always Rises

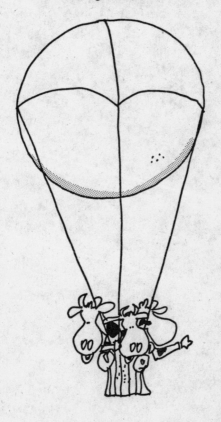

The cream of the crop will rise to the top: Traits and characteristics of those who achieve and become the best in their fields....

Ability

Ability is what will get you to the top if the boss has no daughter.

———

Ability without ambition is like a car without a motor.

———

Executive ability is the talent for deciding something quickly and getting someone else to do it.

The one thing most men can do better than anyone else is to read their own handwriting.

———

No man is fully accomplished until he has acquired the ability to attend to his own business.

Action

Do something. Either lead, follow, or get out of the way.

Adversity

Adversity introduces a man to himself.

———

Graduation from the university of adversity will help prepare a man for a life of diversity.

———

God brings men into deep waters not to drown them, but to cleanse them—*Aighey.*

———

If you want a place in the sun, you have to expect some blisters.

After crosses and losses, men grow humbler and wiser—*Benjamin Franklin.*

Adversity: Gathering clouds putting on their thunderwear.

God gets His best soldiers out of the highlands of affliction—*Charles Spurgeon.*

A smooth sea never made a skillful mariner.

Advice

He who is old should give advice; he who is young should take it.

The reason God made woman last was that He didn't want any advice while creating man.

Most people want to serve God—but only in an advisory capacity.

Good advice is no better than poor advice unless you follow it.

_____

Advice to men over 50: Keep an open mind and a closed refrigerator.

Ambition

Small boy's ambition: I want to grow up to be a farmer so I can get paid for not raising spinach!

_____

Ambition never gets anywhere until it forms a partnership with work.

_____

He who has plenty of push gets along very well without pull.

_____

Ambition without determination has no destination.

_____

Every man has a secret ambition—to outsmart horses, fish, and women.

If more husbands had self-starters, fewer wives would have to be cranks.

The average man's ambition is to be able to afford what he's spending.

Brain

The brain is no stronger than its weakest think.

Always remember that a man is not rewarded for having brains, but for using them.

Be sure your brain is in gear before you engage your mouth.

The most underdeveloped territory in the world lies under your hat.

You aren't what you think you are; what you think you are.

If there's a substitute for brains it has to be silence.

———————

It's unfortunate that rusty brains do not squeak.

Caution

Watch your step; everyone else does.

———————

Caution is the eldest child of wisdom—*Victor Hugo*.

———————

A cautious man is one who hasn't let a woman pin anything on him since he was a baby.

———————

Be cautious: What you forget for a moment you may remember for a lifetime.

———————

Be careful as you slide down the banister of life lest you get a splinter in your career.

———————

A man never knows how careful he can be until he buys a new car or wears white shoes.

It's all right to be cautious—but even a turtle never gets anywhere until he sticks his head out.

Change

Never swap horses while crossing a stream.

———————

A wise man changes his mind; a fool never does.

———————

Accept what you cannot change; change what you cannot accept.

———————

The world changes so fast that you couldn't stay wrong all the time if you tried.

Character

Character is easier kept than recovered.

———————

Character is what you are in the dark.

———————

Character is what you really are; reputation is what others believe you to be.

Reputation is what you need to get a job; character is what you need to keep it.

————

Have character—don't be one!

————

A pat on the back develops character if it is administered young enough, often enough, and low enough.

Cheerfulness

Cheerfulness will open a door when other keys fail.

————

Cheerfulness greases the axles of the world.

————

A cheerful face is nearly as good for an invalid as healthy weather.

————

Some people are able to spread cheer wherever they don't go.

————

Cheerfulness is contagious, but don't wait to catch it from others. Be a carrier!

Common Sense

It's a pity that common sense is such an uncommon commodity.

———

Being almost creamed by the neighborhood bully "brought him to his milk" (brought him to his senses).

———

The man who strays away from common sense will end up dead! (Proverbs 21:16).

———

Love quickens all the senses—except common sense.

———

It's a thousand times better to have common sense without an education than to have an education without common sense.

———

Horse sense means stable thinking.

———

Horse sense vanishes when you begin to feel your oats.

Horse sense is what keeps a woman from becoming a nag.

Conscience

Conscience keeps more people awake than coffee.

———

Conscience is like a baby—it has to go to sleep before you can.

———

Conscience is a device that doesn't keep you from doing something; it just keeps you from enjoying it.

———

Conscience is that inner voice that warns you that someone is looking.

———

Conscience is what makes you tell your wife before someone else does.

———

Conscience is a playback of the still small voice that told you not to do it in the first place.

There is no pillow so soft as a clear conscience—
French proverb.

———

A good conscience is a continual Christmas—
Benjamin Franklin.

Cooperation

No one can whistle a symphony; it takes an orchestra
to play it.

———

Cooperation solves many problems. Even freckles
make a nice coat of tan when they all get together.

———

Who passed the ball to you when you scored?

———

Cooperate! Remember the banana? Every time it
leaves the bunch it gets skinned.

———

If you don't think cooperation is necessary, watch
what happens to a wagon if one wheel comes off.

Criticism

If you're not big enough to stand criticism, you're too small to be praised.

———————

Two things are bad for the heart: running up stairs and running down people.

———————

Don't refuse to accept criticism; get all the help you can (Proverbs 23:12).

———————

People who cannot stand the heat should stay out of the kitchen.

———————

Critics are people who go places and boo things.

———————

Have you ever noticed that most knocking is done by folks who don't know how to ring the bell?

Diplomacy

A diplomat is a man who can make his wife believe she would look fat in a fur coat.

A diplomatic husband said to his wife: How do you expect me to remember your birthday when you never look any older?

———

Diplomacy is the art of handling a porcupine without disturbing the quills.

———

Diplomacy is the ability to take something and make the other fellow believe he is giving it away.

———

Diplomacy is the art of letting someone else have your own way.

———

Diplomacy is the ability to say "Nice Doggie" until you can find a stick.

———

Tact is the ability to give a person a shot in the arm without letting him feel the needle.

———

Tact is powdering your own no's.

Arch Ward says that tact is the ability to shut your mouth before someone else wants to.

Discipline

Lots of us can remember when a wayward child was straightened up by being bent over.

When youth start to sow their wild oats, it's time for parents to start the thrashing machine.

To live a disciplined life, and to accept the results of that discipline as the will of God—that is the mark of a man—*Tom Landry*.

He who is living without discipline is exposed to grievous ruin—*Thomas à Kempis*.

Discipline is the refining fire by which talent becomes ability.

Human beings have will power while mules have won't power.

One sure way to test your willpower is to see a friend with a black eye and not ask any questions.

Enthusiasm

A wise man said that enthusiasm is nothing but faith with a tin can tied to its tail.

––––––

He who has no fire in himself cannot ignite others.

––––––

If it were as easy to raise enthusiasm as it is suspicion, just think what could be accomplished!

––––––

Enthusiasm extinguishes the gloom in the room—*Frank Tyger*.

––––––

Enthusiasm can achieve in one day what takes reasoning centuries.

Experience

Experience is the name we give our mistakes.

Past experience should be a guidepost—not a hitching post.

Some people profit by their experiences; others never recover from them.

One reason experience is such a good teacher is that she doesn't allow any drop-outs.

Experience is what makes your mistakes so familiar.

We learn from experience. A man never wakes up his second baby just to see it smile.

Experience may be the best teacher, but she's not the prettiest.

Failure (Overcoming)

Our greatest glory is not in never failing, but in rising every time we fall.

A college boy sent home a telegram saying, "Mom! Have failed everything! Prepare Pop!"

The reply came the next day, "Pop prepared! Prepare yourself!"

———

A man can fail many times but he isn't a failure until he begins to blame someone else.

———

Failure is the path of least persistence.

———

Ninety-nine percent of the failures come from people who have the habit of making excuses.

———

Failure is not necessarily missing the target, but aiming too low.

Faith

Faith is not a pill you swallow but a muscle you use.

Sorrow looks back. Worry looks around. Faith looks up.

_____

Faith is belief with legs on it.

_____

Feed your faith and your doubts will starve to death.

_____

If doubt overtakes you, stop for a faith lift.

Goals

There are more ways of killing a cat than by choking it with cream.

_____

The three great essentials to achieve anything worthwhile are first, hard work; second, stick-to-itiveness; third, common sense—*Thomas Edison*.

_____

It's more important to know where you're going than to see how fast you can get there.

Do all the good you can,
By all the means you can,
In all the ways you can,
At all the times you can,
To all the people you can,
As long as ever you can.

—*John Wesley*

Where you go hereafter depends on what you go after here.

Find a goal for which you are willing to exchange a piece of your life.

Make sure the things you are living for are worth dying for.

Hope

The best bridge between hope and despair is often a good night's sleep.

Life without hope is a life without meaning.

Hope is the anchor of the soul, the stimulus to action, and the incentive to achievement.

————

Lost hope is the undertaker's best friend.

————

Curiosity is just another word for hope.

————

Hope is faith holding out its hand in the dark.

Humor

Humor is to life what shock absorbers are to automobiles.

————

The best sense of humor belongs to the person who can laugh at himself.

————

Give me a sense of humor, Lord;
    Give me the grace to see a joke,
To get some happiness from life
    And pass it on to other folk.

Humor is the hole that lets the sawdust out of a stuffed shirt.

———

Humor is the lifebelt we use on life's river.

———

A genuine sense of humor is the pole that adds balance to our steps as we walk the tightrope of life

Imagination

If you want to stimulate your imagination, try fishing.

———

Imagination is what makes you think you're having a wonderful time when you're only spending money.

———

Many a girl who elopes wishes later she had just let her imagination run away with her.

Patience

Like farmers, we need to learn that we can't sow and reap in the same day.

Have patience. If you pluck the blossoms, you must do without the fruit.

Patience is the ability to count down before blasting off.

What a mother should save for a rainy day is patience.

Sign in a Texas country store: Be patient. None of us am perfect.

The trouble with people today is that they want to get to the promised land without going through the wilderness.

This would be a wonderful world if men showed as much patience in all things as they do in waiting for a fish to bite.

Better to be patient on the road than a patient in the hospital.

Charles E. Wilson, former president of General Electric, was once asked by the president of a small company how the experiences of a giant corporation like GE could possibly be useful to the pigmy-size businesses of a small Mid-western city.

Wilson answered by recalling a job he held as a kid. He was employed by a dairy to fill milk bottles by ladling out milk from a very large vat. He ladled milk into pint, quart, half-gallon and gallon bottles—some with different-sized necks.

On his way home after a ten-hour work day, he asked himself what he could possibly be learning from such experience. But, he told the young president, after a week of ladling milk from a large vat into pint bottles, small bottles, medium-sized bottles, and large bottles, one fact remained constant; regardless of the size of the bottle—small, medium or large, the cream always came to the top—*John E. Weinrich in* Reader's Digest.

Prayer

He who says he is an atheist has no one to talk to when he's alone.

———

A small boy said to his best friend, "It may be unconstitutional, but I always pray before an exam."

Sign outside a Dallas church: Last chance to pray before entering the freeway.

———

Let's pray for stronger backs not lighter burdens.

———

Life is fragile—handle with prayer.

———

Pray hardest when it's hardest to pray.

———

Ask, and you will be given what you ask for. Seek, and you will find. Knock and the door will be opened (Matthew 7:7).

Preparation

There are four steps to accomplishment: Plan purposefully; prepare prayerfully; proceed positively; and pursue persistently.

———

Today's preparation determines tomorrow's achievement.

Luck is what happens when preparation meets opportunity.

————

Hope for the best, and be ready for the worst.

————

Get ready for eternity. You're going to spend a lot of time there.

————

No farmer ever plowed a field by turning it over in his mind.

Self-control

Good advice not often taken: No! thyself.

————

The best time to keep your shirt on is when you're hot under the collar.

————

Self-control is giving up smoking cigarettes; extreme self-control is not telling anybody about it.

The man who loses his head is usually the last one to miss it.

————

Have you ever noticed how self-control comes in handy when you're eating salted peanuts?

————

Women in supermarkets should exercise shelf-control!

Trust

In God we trust, all others pay cash.

————

Men who trust God are men who can be trusted.

————

When a train goes through a tunnel and it gets dark, you don't throw away your ticket and jump off. You sit still and trust the engineer—*Corrie ten Boom.*

Values

The things in life that count most are the things that can't be counted.

Be slow in choosing friends, slower in changing them.

———

Friendships will last if they are put first.

———

Money can build a house, but it takes love to make it a home.

———

Don't buy it for a song—unless you're sure you know what the pitch is.

———

A Bible stored in the mind is worth a dozen stored in the bottom of a trunk.

———

The trouble with teaching a child the value of a dollar is you have to do it almost every week.

Work

The only workout some folks get is jumping to conclusions, running down their friends, side-stepping responsibilities, and pushing their luck.

The world is full of willing people; some willing to work, the rest willing to let them—*Robert Frost*.

I owe, I owe, it's off to work I go!

Footprints in the sands of time are made by **workboots**.

Salesman: This machine will cut your work in half.

Customer: Great! I'll take two!

If you can't cut the mustard, don't pick up the knife.

Even a mosquito doesn't get a slap on the back until he starts to work.

Wisdom

The door to wisdom swings on hinges of common sense and uncommon thoughts—*William Ward*.

Intelligence: Spotting a flaw in the boss's character.
Wisdom: Not mentioning it.

———————

Wisdom is what you do with what you know.

———————

Wisdom: An open mind and a closed mouth.

———————

God, grant me the serenity to accept the things I cannot change; the courage to change the things I can; and the wisdom to know the difference—
Reinhold Niebuhr.

———————

We're too soon old and too late wise.

———————

The wisest man remembers that to catch a mouse you starve a cat.

———————

As man grows wiser, he talks less and says more.

A wise man restrains his anger and overlooks insults. This is to his credit (Proverbs 19:11).

———————

Speak when you are angry and you'll make the best speech you'll ever regret.

———————

As the churning of cream yields butter, and a blow to the nose causes bleeding, so anger causes quarrels (Proverbs 30:33).

———————

Whenever you are angry, be assured that it is not only a present evil, but that you have increased a habit—*Epictetus*.

———————

The greatest remedy for anger is delay. For every minute you are angry you lose 60 seconds of happiness.

———————

Anger is only one letter short of danger.

———————

Some people are like buttons; always popping off at the wrong time.

Cream Puff

A weakling; a sissy; an effeminate person.

_____

Once a cream puff makes up his mind, he's full of indecision.

_____

He does everything the *herd* way.

_____

He's so nervous, he keeps coffee awake.

_____

He's as spineless as a chocolate eclair.

_____

They call him "Jigsaw." Every time he's faced with a problem, he goes to pieces.

_____

He's just found a job that takes a lot of guts—he strings tennis racquets.

_____

He's more nervous than a turkey in November.

He's as jumpy and fidgety as a long-tailed cat in a room full of rocking chairs.

———

He even says "Thank You" when an automatic door opens for him.

———

His motto is "It isn't who you know but who you yes."

———

He's the kind of guy who falls for everything and stands for nothing.

———

He's as spineless as spaghetti.

———

He's the sort of namby-pamby who gets lost in a crowd of two.

———

He's the kind of mollycoddle who asks permission to ask permission.

Udder Advice

Udder: faucet on a cow.

_____

The city girl watching the farmer milk a cow: That looks easy, but how do you turn it off?

_____

City boy: Say, Dad, how many kinds of milk are there?

Father: Well, there's evaporated milk, buttermilk, malted milk, and—but why do you wish to know?

City boy: Oh, I'm drawing a picture of a cow, and I want to know how many spigots to put on her.

_____

Dairy owners owe their living to udders.

_____

Udderance: The gift of eloquent speech.

A cow should be milked clean. Not a drop, if it can be avoided, should be left in the udder—that would be udder folly!

Anger

The thunder of angry words "sours the milk of human kindness."

———————

The greatest remedy for anger is delay.

———————

People who are always hitting the ceiling are usually full of hot air.

———————

Hot heads and cold hearts never solve anything.

———————

People, like pins, are useless when they lose their heads.

———————

Our tempers get us into trouble and pride keeps us there.

Anger is the wind that blows out the lamp of intelligence.

———

Charity is the sterilized milk of human kindness.

Babies

There is no finer investment for any community than putting milk into babies—*Winston Churchill*.

———

A baby is God's opinion that the world should go on—*Carl Sandburg*.

———

A perfect example of minority rule is a baby in the house.

———

Babies are angels whose wings grow shorter as their legs grow longer.

———

Babies are little rivets in the bonds of marriage.

Babies: a loud noise at one end and no sense of responsibility at the other.

———————

We buy everything on time. We haven't even paid for the baby yet. As of last Tuesday, we own one leg, one arm, and a navel!

Contentment

He was as "contented as a cow in a corn patch."

———————

A contented man enjoys the scenery on a detour.

———————

Contentment does not mean less work but more cheer.

———————

Contentment is when your earning power equals your yearning power.

———————

It's okay to be content with what you have but never with what you are.

Some people are not content with the milk of human kindness—they want the cream.

———————

There's nothing like a dish towel to wipe that contented look off a husband's face.

———————

All the world lives in two tents: content and discontent.

———————

The tough thing about living alone—you have to sniff the milk before you drink it.

———————

All the good ideas I ever had came to me while I was milking a cow—*Grant Wood*.

———————

The two happiest moments of my life at Bath Farm were the first time I was left to milk Bess on my own, and the first time she came across the pasture when I called her—*Rachel Knappett*.

———————

John Coombs, a Wiltshire, England farmer, bald for 20 years, found hairs sprouting again after one of his cows licked the top of his head!

Purple Cow

I never saw a purple cow,
  I never hope to see one;
But I can tell you, anyhow,
  I'd rather see than be one.
                    —*F. Gelett Burgess*

———

Ah, yes, I wrote "Purple Cow"—
  I'm sorry, now, I wrote it!
But I can tell you anyhow,
  I'll kill you if you quote it.
                    —*F. Gelett Burgess*

Cost of Living

It is better to buy a quart of milk for a dollar than to own and keep a cow.

———

Congress must not improve our lot in life any further. We simply can't afford it.

———

It's now costing us twice as much to live beyond our means as it did 20 years ago.

The way things are now you're lucky if you can make one end meet.

———————

A dollar may not go as far as it used to, but what it lacks in distance it makes up in speed.

———————

Today one can buy ten cents worth of almost anything for 30 cents.

———————

The best way to hear money jingle in your pocket is to "shake a leg."

———————

People who borrow often sorrow.

———————

The trouble with public debt is that private individuals have to pay for it.

———————

If you think you won't be missed, try moving away and leaving a few unpaid bills.

They ought to make it as hard to get into debt as it is to get out.

_____

Next to debt, the hardest thing to get out of is a warm bed on a cold morning.

_____

What you don't owe won't hurt you.

_____

She who uses charge card to buy hat is in debt over her ears.

_____

Blessed are the young, for they shall inherit the national debt—*Herbert Hoover*.

Deception

> Things are seldom what they seem,
> Skim milk masquerades as cream.
> —*W.S. Gilbert*

_____

Deception is a short blanket—if you pull it over your face, you expose your feet.

You can fool some of the people all of the time, and all of the people some of the time, but you cannot fool all of the people all of the time—*Abraham Lincoln.*

———

A truthful witness does not deceive, but a false witness pours out lies (Proverbs 14:5 NIV).

———

Let us endeavor to so live that when we come to die even the undertaker will be sorry—*Mark Twain.*

———

Sometimes he who thinks he's in the groove is only in a rut.

———

Oh, what a tangled web we weave, when first we practice to deceive—*Sir Walter Scott.*

Foolishness

Mooncalf: A fool from birth; a talkative scatterbrain.

When arguing with a fool, be sure he's not doing the same thing.

———————

A fool does at the end what a wise man does at the beginning.

———————

The fool wanders, the wise man travels.

———————

The fool declares: I never make misteaks!

———————

Wise men learn something from fools, but fools learn nothing from wise men.

———————

There's no fool like an old fool—you can't beat experience—*Jacob Braude*.

———————

Stupidity is forever, ignorance can be fixed.

Humility

To be humble to superiors is duty; to equals, courtesy; to inferiors, nobility.

Before retiring to bed, Theodore Roosevelt and his friend the naturalist William Beebe would go out and look at the skies, searching for a tiny patch of light near the constellation of Pegasus. "That is the Spiral Galaxy in Andromeda," they would chant. "It is as large as our Milky Way. It is one of a hundred million galaxies. It consists of one hundred billion suns, each larger than our sun." Then Roosevelt would turn to his companion and say, "Now I think we are small enough. Let's go to bed."

———

Few things are as humbling as a three-way mirror.

———

Those traveling the highway of humility won't be bothered by heavy traffic.

———

Humility is like underwear. We should have it— but not let it show.

Kindness

Don't expect to enjoy life if you keep the milk of human kindness all bottled up.

People who sow seeds of kindness enjoy a perpetual harvest.

If you were arrested for being kind, would enough evidence be found to convict you?

The greatest thing a man can do for his heavenly Father is to be kind to His children.

The milk of human kindness never curdles.

Money will buy a fine dog, but only kindness will make him wag his tail.

Kindness is a language which the deaf can hear and the blind can see.

Laziness

A lazy fellow has trouble all through life; the good man's path is easy! (Proverbs 15:19).

He slept beneath the moon,
   He baked beneath the sun;
He lived a life of going-to-do
   And died with nothing done.

The lazier a man is, the more he plans to do tomorrow.

He's the kind of student with a Cadillac mind but a Pinto performance.

Sunday school teacher: What parable do you like most?

Little Johnny: The one about the multitude that loafs and fishes.

Boss: You're the laziest guy I've ever seen. Don't you do anything quickly?

Ross: Yes, I get tired fast.

Luck

Good luck often has the odor of perspiration about it.

Luck is a wonderful thing—the harder a man works, the more he seems to have of it.

———————

Choice, not chance, determines destiny.

———————

A rabbit's foot is a poor substitute for horse sense.

———————

Nothing improves a man's luck like fish that are in a biting mood.

———————

You can always tell luck from ability by its duration.

———————

Industry is the mother of success—luck, a distant relative.

———————

Luck is what happens when preparation meets opportunity.

Milking a Laugh

He who laughs lasts.

He knew how to get more laughs than the part deserved.

———————

Will Rogers said, "We are all here for a spell; get all the good laughs you can."

———————

Don't take life too seriously; laugh a lot. You'll never get out of it alive.

———————

A happy face means a glad heart; a sad face means a breaking heart (Proverbs 15:13).

———————

A good laugh is the best medicine, whether you are sick or not. Fortune smiles on the man who can laugh at himself.

———————

Laughter is the sun that drives winter from the human face—*Victor Hugo*.

———————

A laugh is worth a hundred groans in any market.

Optimism

A spilled glass of milk flows in the direction of the most expensive object.

———

When confronted with a Goliath-sized problem, which way do you respond: "He's too big to hit," or, like David, "He's too big to miss"?

———

Your future is as bright as the promises of God.

———

If it were not for the optimist, the pessimist would never know how happy he isn't.

———

An optimist is a fisherman who takes along a camera.

———

The optimist says his glass is half full; the pessimist says his glass is half empty.

———

The woman who starts putting on her shoes when the preacher says, "And now in conclusion," is a real optimist.

Pessimism

He who can look at the land of milk and honey and see only calories and cholesterol is a pessimist.

A pessimist is a person who looks at the world through woes-colored glasses—*Colmes*.

A hopeless pessimist is always building dungeons in the air.

A pessimist is someone who feels bad when he feels good for fear he will feel worse when he feels better.

Pessimism is contagious—you can get it by listening attentively to the six-o'clock news.

Most pessimists are seasick during the entire voyage of life.

Pessimists discount their blessings; optimists count theirs.

Regret

Where two or three are gathered together someone spills his milk—*Tom Mullen*.

———

The guy who said there's no use crying over spilt milk said it back in the days when it was six cents a quart.

———

If you must cry over spilt milk, condense it.

———

Spilt milk: Anything which once misused or abused cannot be recovered.

———

Between tomorrow's dream and yesterday's regret is today's opportunity.

———

You can't have rosy thoughts about the future when your mind is full of the blues about the past.

———

A kindness put off till tomorrow may become only a bitter regret.

Be grateful for what you have, not regretful for what you haven't.

———

Anger is a state that starts with madness and ends with regret.

———

I regret often that I have spoken; never that I have been silent.

———

Don't spend the last half of your life regretting the first half.

———

For of all sad words of tongue or pen,
The saddest are these: It might have been!

———

Make it a rule of life never to regret and never look back. Regret is an appalling waste of energy; you can't build on it; it's only good for wallowing in—*Katherine Mansfield*.

———

When you can think of yesterday without regret and tomorrow without fear, you are closing in on real contentment.

Service

The milkman alone is enough to redeem the night from its undeserved evil reputation. A cartload of pasteurized milk for nurslings at four o'clock in the morning represents more service to civilization than a cartful of bullion on its way from the Subtreasury to the vaults of a national bank five hours later—*Simeon Strunsky.*

Do you see a man skilled in his work? He will serve before kings; he will not serve before obscure men (Proverbs 22:29 NIV).

Fortunate is the person who has learned that the most certain way to "get" is to first "give" through some sort of useful service.

Service is love in working clothes.

Life is like a game of tennis—you can't win without serving.

Did you hear about the manicurist and the chiropodist who got married? They waited on each other—hand and foot.

Silence

Though she wore a loud bell, the cow had made the discovery that if she stood perfectly still it would not ring. So Sylvia had to hunt for her (in the bushes) until she found her—*Sarah Orne Jewett.*

If silence is golden, not many people can be arrested for hoarding.

The ability to speak several languages is valuable, but the art of keeping silent in one is precious.

The man of few words and settled mind is wise; therefore, even a fool is thought to be wise when he is silent. It pays him to keep his mouth shut (Proverbs 17:27,28).

It is better to be silent and be considered a fool than to speak and remove all doubt.

"I have never been hurt by anything I didn't say," commented Calvin Coolidge.

If there's a substitute for brains, it must be silence.

Slowness

"Get off and milk it!"—an expression shouted at someone who is riding a bicycle slowly.

———

Manager to slow-moving office boy: I don't know how we're going to get along without you but starting Monday we're going to give it a try.

———

Grandfather is known for always driving well below the speed limit. One Sunday my grandparents were going to attend a family gathering. "Hurry or we'll be late!" Gram repeatedly urged him. He continued on just as slowly.

Finally Gram could take it no longer. "Stop the car, dear, and let me out," she said in her sweetest voice. "I'll run on ahead and tell them we're coming"—*Michelle Johnson in* Reader's Digest.

———

Office sign: If you have nothing to do, please don't do it here.

He did nothing in particular, and did it very well—*W.S. Gilbert.*

Success

He who wants milk should not set himself in the middle of a pasture waiting for a cow to back up to him.

———————

Everyone has his day, and some days last longer than others—*Winston Churchill.*

———————

The secret of success is to be like a duck—smooth and unruffled on top, but paddling like crazy underneath.

———————

The road to success is all uphill.

———————

The road to success is filled with women pushing their husbands along—*Lord Thomas Robert Dewar.*

———————

Nothing succeeds like success—*Alexandre Dumas.*

Of course everybody likes and respects self-made men. It's a great deal better to be made in that way than not to be made at all—*Oliver Wendell Holmes*.

———

Did you hear about the Beverly Hill's barber who climbed the lather to success?

———

Becoming number one is easier than remaining number one—*Bill Bradley*.

———

Success humbles the great man, astonishes the common man, and puffs up the little man.

———

The secret of success is constancy of purpose—*Disraeli*.

———

A man who refuses to admit his mistakes can never be successful. But if he confesses and forsakes them, he gets another chance (Proverbs 28:13).

Did you hear about the fellow who climbed the ladder of success wrong by wrong?

———

The Weakest Think

If you think you are beaten, you are,
If you think you dare not, you don't,
If you'd like to win, but you think you can't
It's almost a cinch that you won't.

If you think you'll lose, you're lost,
For out of the world we find
Success begins with a fellow's will,
It's all in the state of mind.

If you think you're outclassed, you are.
You've got to think high to rise,
You've got to be sure of yourself, you see,
Before you can win a prize.

The victories of life do not always go
To the swifter or smarter man,
But sooner or later the man who wins
Is the man who thinks he can.

—Author unknown

———

You don't have to lie awake nights to succeed—just stay awake days.

———

A successful man keeps on looking for work after he has found a job.

The Lord has given us two ends,
    They have a common link;
For with the bottom end we sit,
    And with the other think.

Success in life depends upon
    Which end you choose to use.
You'll soon discover this, my friend,
    Heads you win and tails you lose!

———

The toughest thing about success is you've got to keep on being a success—*Irving Berlin*.

———

It takes 20 years to make an overnight success—*Eddie Cantor*.

———

A successful man is the one who can lay a firm foundation with the bricks that others throw at him—*David Brinkley*.

———

Success often comes from taking a misstep in the right direction.

———

The cow that's first up gets the first of the dew—*Scottish proverb*.

Upstream

The easy roads are crowded and
  The level roads are jammed.
The pleasant little rivers
  With the drifting folks are crammed.
But off yonder where it's rocky,
  Where you get the better view,
You will find the ranks are thinning,
  And the travelers are few.

Where the going's smooth and pleasant
  You will always find the throng,
For the many—more's the pity—
  Seem to like to drift along.
But the steeps that call for courage
  And the task that's hard to do
In the end results in glory
  For the never wavering few!
          —*Author Unknown*

———

The laggard cow gets the sour grass—*Danish proverb.*

———

The early bird gets the worm.

———

He who wants to trick the fox must rise early.

It is the early rising and the well-spending of the day that is the unbeatable combination to success.

———

People who do a good day's work seldom have to worry about a good night's sleep.

———

He who wakes up and finds himself famous hasn't been asleep.

———

Bull's eye: the central colored disk on a target.

———

People who aim at nothing are sure to hit it.

———

Before you can score you must first have a goal.

———

Aim high but stay on the level.

———

Climb high, climb far; your aim the sky, your goal the star.

There's no sense aiming at the target with no arrow in your bow.

———————

Men with a good aim in life must know when to pull the trigger.

———————

Success comes from having the right aim as well as the right ammunition.

Truth

> Truth, like milk, arrives in the dark
>   But even so, wise dogs don't bark.
> Only mongrels make it hard
>   For the milkman to come up the yard.
>   —*Christopher Morley*

———————

A lie goes around the world while truth is putting its boots on.

———————

A good thing about telling the truth is that you don't have to remember what you said.

Just why do men tell lies about each other when the plain truth would be bad enough?

———

Men occasionally stumble over the truth, but most of them pick themselves up and hurry off as if nothing had happened.

———

Watch out for a half-truth; you might get hold of the wrong half.

———

Those who stretch the truth usually find that it snaps back.

Work

Cows do not "give" milk. If you are wiley and strong and ruthless, you can have it for the taking—*J.P. McEvoy*.

———

One thing you can learn by watching the clock is that it passes the time by keeping its hands busy.

———

Hard work means prosperity; only a fool idles away his time (Proverbs 12:11).

The more steam you put into your work, the louder you can whistle when the work is done.

The only place where success comes before work is in the dictionary.

Genius is about 2 percent inspiration and 98 percent perspiration—*Thomas Edison*.

Helpmate

He's *glad* to wash the windows;
  He rather *likes* to paint;
As anyone can plainly see,
  I'm living with a saint.

He volunteers to wash the floors
  Without a word from me—
Nor does he find such work a threat
  To masculinity.

When he is home he lends a hand
  In everything I do;
But—would that he were thirty-odd
  Instead of only two!

                    —*Claris Miller*

Do you know a hard-working man? He shall be successful and stand before kings! (Proverbs 22:29).

———————

I like work; it fascinates me. I can sit and look at it for hours. I love to keep it by me; the idea of getting rid of it nearly breaks my heart—*Jerome*.

———————

I never did anything worth doing by accident, nor did any of my inventions come by accident; they came by work—*Thomas Edison*.

———————

Work brings profit; talk brings poverty! (Proverbs 14:23).

———————

Success is sweet, but its secret is sweat. Fortunately, no one has ever drowned himself in sweat.

———————

God gives us the ingredients for our daily bread, but we must do the baking.

———————

Some people remind us of French bread—one long loaf.

Our country's number one energy crisis is Monday morning.

Hysterical (Historical) Milk Section

Milk run: an easy military aerial mission, usually a bombing mission—easy either because no opposition is encountered or because the distance covered is short.

———

Milk wagon: a police wagon or truck used to transport arrested people to jail.

———

Milk run: a train that stops at every point to pick up milk cans or other goods.

———

Milk shake: introduced in the late 1880's as a sturdy, healthful, eggnog type of drink served first as a tonic for infants and invalids as well as a treat.

———

Malted milk shake: arrived in the early 1900's when malt was added to milk shakes. It became known as a "shake" or "malt."

Milk ranches of the 1850's became dairy farms in the 1870's. Milk trains, then milk cars, transported milk to the cities starting in 1919.

———

Milkman: delivered milk on milk routes in milk wagons. In 1830, he poured milk into family milk can left outside the door.

———

Milk maid: a woman or girl who milks cows or works in a dairy.

———

Milksop: a weak, timorous fellow; sissy; yellow-belly, crybaby.

———

Milk toast: a dish of buttered toast served in hot milk. In 1857, sugar or cinnamon was added—"an American dish."

A Jug Full of Creamy Crazies

A man ordered coffee without cream. The waitress, new and not too bright, replied, "I'm sorry, Sir, we're all out of cream but I can give it to you without milk!"

The friendly cow, all red and white,
  I love with all my heart:
She gives me cream with all her might
  To eat with apple-tart.
— *Robert Louis Stevenson*

———————

Lana: What do you feed your pet frog?

Dana: Croakers and cream.

———————

Farmer: Stop it! Stop it! Why are you beating the feet of the cows like that and making them jump up and down?

Freddy: I'm trying to make a milk shake.

———————

Farmer Smith has just invented a new device which enables him to count his cows in the field quickly. He calls his invention a cowculator.

———————

D. L. Moody once said, "Most people talk cream and live skim milk."

Cream

To severely damage, wreck, ruin, or total an automobile.

Sign visible to drivers entering St. John, Indiana: Drive carefully. See St. John, not St. Peter.

———

Hundreds of nuts hold a car together but one can scatter it all over the highway.

———

People who weave through traffic may wind up in stiches.

———

Young drivers who drive too fast into the next county may wind up in the next world.

———

Always try to drive so that your license will expire before you do.

———

Drive cautiously and carefully, and don't insist on your rites.

———

It's better to be a few minutes late down here than years too early up there.

Graffiti from the Creamery

Keep death off the road, drive on the sidewalk.

———

On a jalopy: This car may be old—but it's in front of you and it's paid for.

———

This car has reached middle-age—it doesn't want to go over 40.

———

On a severely creamed car: Next dents, please!

———

I bought a Toyota because I had a yen for one.

———

My Fiat is killing me

———

Drive carefully—the life you save may owe us money.

———

The only marks some drivers make in life are skid marks.

Drive defensively and sensibly. If you don't, your present car may last you a lifetime.

———————

Let's not meet by accident!

———————

If your children want to take driving lessons, don't stand in their way.

———————

Seat belts are not as confining as wheelchairs.

———————

One way to make people slow down in their driving would be to call it work.

———————

Famous last words: I wonder how much this car will do?

———————

There are two finishes for automobiles: lacquer and liquor.

———————

The hand that lifts the cup that cheers, should not be used to shift the gears.

Ice Cream Social

"Mother," said the little girl, "May I have a dime for the old man who is outside crying?"

"Yes, dear," said the mother, "but what is he crying about?"

"The old man is crying," said the little girl, "'Ice cream cones are ten cents!'"

Did you hear about the new pasta diet? Just walk pasta bakery without stopping. Walk pasta candy store without stopping. Walk pasta ice cream shop without stopping.

Ice cream: Freezy kid stuff—*W.E. Piece*.

Did you hear about the farmer who kept his cows in the ice house so they could make ice cream?

"Won't you have a second helping of ice cream?" the hostess at dinner asked Helen. "Do have some more," the hostess insisted.

Young Helen answered: "Mother told me to say, 'No thank you,' but I don't think she could have known how small that first helping was going to be!"

It was unseasonably warm that day, even for sunny Los Angeles. A little girl came into the ice cream store with her money clutched in her hand. Before she could order, the sharp-featured clerk told her to go outside, read the sign, and stay out until she put on some shoes. A big man followed her out of the store.

I watched as she stood out front and looked at the sign. NO BARE FEET. Then, with tears rolling down her cheeks, she turned and started to walk away. The big man sat down on the sidewalk, took off his number twelve shoes, and set them down by the door.

"You won't be able to walk in these," he said. "But if you just sort of slide along, you can get your ice cream soda." Then he lifted the little girl and set her down with her feet in the shoes.

"Take your time," he added. "I get tired of moving those shoes around, so I'll just sit here and rest."

He was a big man, all right. Big belly, big feet, big heart—*Evelyn Pierce*.

Did you ever wonder why that delicious dessert is called an ice cream "sundae"?

A popular explanation is that in the late 1800s, local laws forbade the sale of soda on the Sabbath.

To attract the Sunday crowd, ice cream parlors started serving sodaless ice cream and fruit concoctions, which people began calling "sundays." Later the parlors altered the word's spelling, hoping to change the dish's image to that of an everyday treat—*Douglas B. Smith in* Reader's Digest.

———

John: Why are you eating your ice cream so fast?

Jack: My mother just called me for lunch.

Courage

One man with courage makes a majority.

———

Don't be afraid to go out on a limb—that's where the fruit is!

———

Actually there's only a slight difference between keeping your chin up and sticking your neck out—but it's a difference worth knowing.

A man's courage can sustain his broken body, but when courage dies, what hope is left? (Proverbs 18:14).

———————

A friend of mine was driving on a long stretch of California highway when he became the tailender in a line of cars traveling at precisely 53 miles per hour.

After a while, he pulled out and gradually passed the rest at 57 miles per hour.

The siren sounded and the lights blinked.

My friend sighed and pulled over.

The officer walked up, "When I finished my shift this afternoon," said the patrolman, "I bought a quart of ice cream to take home to the family. Then I got a call to stay on duty.

"The ice cream is going to melt, so I decided to give it to the first motorist who had the courage to pass me."

He handed over the ice cream with a "Good day, sir," and returned to his patrol duties.

———————

Courage is fear that has said its prayers.

———————

Progress always involves a certain amount of risk. After all, you can't steal second base with one foot on first.

There was a little quarterback who played in a small college. He had just become a Christian and did not know how to tell others of his newfound happiness. The only way he knew to let them know was to carry a Bible to class with him. After he had carried it for a few days one of the big tackles came up to him and said: "What's the matter, have you gone soft and become a Christian?" The little quarterback looked up, took the Bible and held it out to him, and said: "If you think it's easy, here, you carry it."

———

It takes courage to stand up and speak, as well as to sit down and listen.

———

Keep your chin up and your knees down.

———

Did you hear about the military inductee who, when asked if he had any physical defects, replied, "No guts!"

Fresh from
the Churn

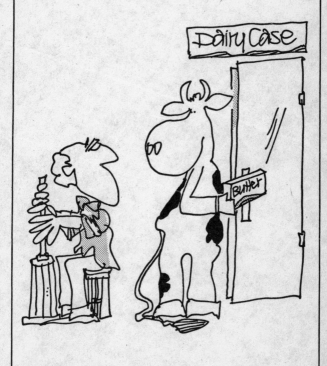

I never had a piece of toast
   Particularly long and wide,
But fell upon the sanded floor,
   And always on the buttered side.

———

The butter was so hard, the knife slipped and I buttered the bread up to my elbow.

———

There are those who cast their bread upon the waters, hoping it will be returned to them toasted and buttered.

———

The hardness of the butter is in direct proportion to the softness of the bread.

During my weekly visit to the beauty salon, the conversation in the shop turned to how both men and women were beginning a courtship and marrying soon after a spouse died instead of waiting, as was once the custom.

"I know exactly what my husband will do after I die," I said. "He will marry the first woman who brings him a pan of cornbread."

All was quiet a moment; then one of the beauticians turned to me and asked, "Does he like butter on it?"—*Maureen Childress in* Reader's Digest.

Keep Paddling

Two frogs fell into a bucket of cream,
    And must paddle to keep afloat,
But one soon tired and sank to rest
    With a gurgling sound in his throat.

The other paddled away all night,
    And not a croak did he utter;
And with the coming of morning light
    He rode on an island of butter.

The flies came thick to his island home
    And made him a breakfast snappy;
The milkmaid shirked and upset the pail,
    And froggie hopped away happy.

A moral we find in this simple rhyme,
    And hasten at once to apply;
Success will come in the most difficult time,
    If we paddle and never say die.

—*Author unknown*

Fat-Steps to the Fat Farm

Overweight: What happens when you take the butter with the sweet.

———

Did you hear about the lady who went to the fat farm and discovered the program really worked? The first day alone she was $500 lighter.

———

Let's be diplomatic about this. I am *not* fat! Let's just say I suffer from overbite.

———

Fat is nature's way of explaining to you why your food bill is $200 a week.

———

If your father weighs 250 pounds and your mother weighs 230 pounds and you weigh 210 pounds—you're following in their fat-steps!

———

My wife is a little concerned about my weight. So am I. Yesterday we had to let out the tape measure.

Diets are for people who are thick and tired of it.

———————

If at first you don't recede, diet, diet again.

Butter-Up!

Defined: butter. n. Flattery. Colloq. v.t. = butter up.

———————

Did you hear about the little cannibal boy who was expelled from school? They caught him buttering up the teacher!

———————

A slanderer is a guy who says things behind your back he wouldn't say to your face.

A flatterer is a guy who says things to your face he wouldn't say behind your back.

———————

'Tis an old maxim in the schools,
    That flattery's the food of fools;
Yet now and then your men of wit
    Will condescend to take a bit—*Swift*.

Did you hear about the suitor who soft-soaped his girl until she couldn't see for the suds?

———————

Imitation is the sincerest form of flattery.

———————

Tell her she's too smart to be flattered—and flattered she is!

———————

He who has butterfingers should not try to climb the rope.

Butterflies

The speaker had such a severe case of butterflies in his stomach he broke out in a cold sweat. "When I got here tonight, both God and I knew what I was going to say. Now only God knows!"

———————

Our anxiety does not empty tomorrow of its sorrows, but only empties today of its strength—*Spurgeon*.

Cast all your anxiety on him because he cares for you (1 Peter 5:7 NIV).

———————

Man spends too much time reasoning on the past, complaining of the present, and trembling for the future.

———————

Feed your faith and your apprehensions will starve to death.

———————

When fear knocks at your door, send faith to answer.

———————

Prayer

Give us, Lord, a bit o' sun,
    A bit o' work, and a bit o' fun;
Give us all in the struggle and splutter,
    Our daily bread and a bit o' butter.

Give us, Lord, a chance to be
    Our goodly best, brave, wise, and free,
Our goodly best for ourselves and others,
    Till all men learn to live as brothers.
        —*From an Old English Inn*

A merchant went to a farmer to get a pound of butter. The farmer insisted on swapping the butter for a pair of woolen socks. The merchant went home and reported this to his wife.

"We have a woolen bedspread," she said. "I'll unravel it and knit a pair of socks." So she proceeded to make the pair of socks, and the merchant exchanged them for a pound of butter.

When the merchant needed more butter, his wife would unravel more of the bedspread and knit more socks to be exchanged for the butter. Finally one day she had enough wool left for only one sock. The merchant took it to the farmer and asked for a half pound of butter for it.

"No, I'll give you a full pound," said the farmer. "You see, I really don't wear socks. My wife unravels the wool and uses it for knitting a bedspread, and there's just enough in this one sock to finish it."

Till the Cows Come Home

In the rural district where a friend once attended school, time spent on the school bus presented a problem because he had to get home early to start milking the cows. So he went to the assistant principal, seeking permission to drive his car to school.

The assistant principal, who had just moved to the rural area from the city, listened to the problem, thought a moment, and rendered his decision: "You may drive to school for now, but once the milking season is over you'll have to take the bus again."

A farmer works from daybreak till backbreak.

A farmer is a man who believes in the eight-hour day: eight hours in the forenoon and eight hours in the afternoon.

Sunday school teacher: What do you think the "land flowing with milk and honey" will be like?

Student: Sticky!

———————

A farmer kept a prize cow in a pasture through which a railroad track ran. Each day at the same time a freight train barreled by. One day after the train had gone, the farmer discovered his cow was missing. He promptly sued the railroad.

The railroad hired a young lawyer, and just before the case came to trial, the attorney bargained with the farmer, getting him to settle for half of what he had demanded. Proud of his achievement, the lawyer boasted as he handed over the settlement check to the farmer: "You really had me worried. I didn't have any witnesses. The engineer was asleep, and so was the brakeman. You could have won the whole amount."

"Well, young fella," the farmer said as he pocketed the check, "you had me worried, too. You see, that crazy cow came home this morning"—*Dan Glickman in* Reader's Digest.

———————

The farmer doesn't go to work. He wakes up every morning surrounded by it.

One thing farmers aren't raising enough of is farmhands.

———

Any girl who wants to be sure she will never be unemployed should marry a farmer.

———

Dairy farming: You raise more feed to make more milk so you can have more money to buy more land so you can have more cows and raise more feed....

———

Farm: A section of land on which, if you get up early enough mornings and work late enough nights, you'll make money—if you strike oil.

———

The hardest thing to learn about dairy farming is getting up at five to milk cows.

———

He bought a farm five miles long and two inches wide. He plans to raise spaghetti.

———

A farmer is outstanding in his field.

I had trouble understanding why my country-reared husband wasn't as excited by beautiful sunrises as I was. Then a friend, also raised in the country, offered this explanation: "He probably remembers too many sunrises over the rump of a mule"—*Agnes Hulsey in* Reader's Digest.

———

The older generation thought nothing of getting up at five every morning to milk the cows—and the younger generation doesn't think much of it either.

———

You'll never make your dreams come true by oversleeping.

———

If you love sleep, you will end in poverty. Stay awake, work hard, and there will be plenty to eat! (Proverbs 20:13).

———

Hay: Something it is smart to make between the time you crawl out of it and the time you hit it again—*June Collier*.

———

Ideas not put into practice are merely dreams.

Grandfather had a farm, his son has a garden, and his grandson has a can opener.

The kind of vegetables we enjoy are those the cow eats before we eat the cow.

A city boy spent his first night on the farm. Awakened much earlier than usual by the activity around him, he remarked sleepily, "It doesn't take long to stay here all night, does it?"

Jones: Look at that bunch of cows.

Smith: Not bunch—herd!

Jones: Heard what?

Smith: Herd of cows.

Jones: Sure, I've heard of cows.

Smith: I mean—a cow herd!

Jones: What do I care if a cow heard? I didn't say anything I shouldn't have!

Farmer (carrying a milk pail and approaching a cow): Well, Elsie, what will it be today—milk or chopped steak?

A farmer wrote to Sears, Roebuck and Co.: Please send me one of them milking machines you advertise on page 678 and if it's any good I'll send you a check for it.

The following reply was received promptly: Send us the check and if it is any good we will send you the machine.

Socialism: You give one of your two cows to your neighbor.

Communism: You give both of your cows to the government.

Capitalism: You sell one cow and buy a bull.

Three Acres and a Cow

We're all to have a bit of land,
  And learn to speed the plough,
And live forever happy
  On three acres and a cow.
        —*Jesse Collings, 1886*

The public buys its opinions as it buys its milk, on the principle that it is cheaper to do this than to keep a cow—*Samuel Butler*.

The farmer's rosy-cheeked, bobbed-haired daughter came striding along the lane from the farmhouse. She was clad in grimy overalls; from the pockets bulged bunches of cottonwaste and sundry tools. One hand carried a bag of tools, the other a wrench.

"Where are you going, my pretty maid?" jokingly asked the squire's son, who met her.

"I'm going a-milking, sir," she said.
The squire's son looked surprised.

"But the tools—what are they for?" he asked.

"Trouble," sighed the girl, "with the dashed new milking machine that father has just installed in the cowshed."

———

My sister, who is married to a dairy farmer, was complaining to him about all the drop-in company they have. Her husband couldn't understand why she minded a few extra people at mealtime.

"How would you feel," she said, "if every time someone dropped in they brought five extra cows for you to milk?"—*Marcia A. Luther in* Reader's Digest.

———

This sign appeared on a Sullivan County, New York barn: Trespassers shot—if missed, prosecuted!

Did you ever wonder why so many barns are painted red?

In the mid-19th century, some American farmers found they could make a cheap and long-lasting wood covering from red iron oxide, skim milk, lime, and linseed oil. This mixture gave the barn a bright-red color. Its use became so widespread that, by the late 1800s, red had become traditional for barns—*Douglas B. Smith in* Reader's Digest.

Sign painted on a milk truck: Don't be quart short!

Mrs. Mountaineer: Paw, why're ye wearing all those clothes to paint the barn?

Mr. Mountaineer: I'm just following the directions on the can. It says to do a good job you have to put on three coats.

A young chap applying for work on a dairy farm was asked by the farmer, "Do you have any bad habits? Do you smoke, drink, or stay out late?"

"Oh, no, sir, none of those!" replied the prospective employee. "But I do one thing I think you ought to know about. I use margarine!"

Habits are at first cobwebs, then cables.

A salesman was trying to talk a farmer into buying a bicycle, but was meeting with considerable sales resistance.

"Shucks, I'd sooner spend my money on a cow," said the farmer.

"Ah," replied the salesman, "but think how silly you'd look riding around on a cow."

"Humph!" retorted the farmer. "Not near as silly as I'd look trying to milk a bicycle."

———

When her favorite bull was accidentally shot, Bessie the cow rationalized the situation by thinking that to err is human, but to forgive bovine.

———

An American traveling in Scotland got into a conversation with a local farmer, and in the course of the talk he remarked:

"I guess you haven't heard about the cattle salve we have in the United States. You simply cut off a cow's tail, rub the salve on the stump, and you'll have a new tail on the cow in a week's time."

"Hoot, mon, that's naething. Ye ocht tae see the embrocation we ha'e at the place I coom frame. Ye simply cut a coo's tail aff, rub the salve on the tail, an in a week's time a new coo grows on the auld tail."

A habit is like a soft bed—easy to get into but hard to get out of.

————————

The easiest and best way to break a habit is to drop it.

————————

A wolf may grow old,
  And his hair turn to gray,
But his mind doesn't change
  To his dying day.

————————

An old dairy farmer listened patiently to an overly enthusiastic salesman leafing through a thick manual on scientific dairy farming. Asked to purchase the manual, the farmer drawled, "Son, I don't farm half as good as I know how to already."

————————

"Your methods of cultivation are hopelessly out of date," said the youthful agricultural college graduate to the old farmer. "Why, I'd be astonished if you ever got ten pounds of apples from that tree."

"So would I," replied the farmer. "It's a pear tree!"

On October 8, 1871, a disastrous fire completely burned an area in Chicago of more than three square miles, destroyed more than 17,000 buildings, left 100,000 people homeless, and took 250 lives. According to legend, the fire was caused by a Mrs. O'Leary's cow, who is said to have kicked over a lantern in the barn.

––––––

Knowing without doing is like plowing without sowing.

––––––

Conceit is what makes a little squirt think he's a fountain of knowledge.

––––––

What you learn in youth you do not unlearn in old age.

––––––

Everybody should get at least a high school education—even if they already know everything.

––––––

You have to know the ropes in order to pull the string.

The fellow who knows more than his boss should be careful to conceal it.

———————

Last year I was wandering about at the county fair, curiously inspecting all of the exhibitions. Upon hearing the familiar rambling of an auctioneer, I noticed a large crowd gathering near the barns where livestock are shown. Farm children were selling the calves, pigs, and sheep they had raised themselves. Each child led his or her animal up to the front, described it briefly, and the bidding began.

The next child up was a little girl with a cute lamb. She told how she enjoyed raising it and that the money from selling it would go toward cancer research. The girl went on to say she had leukemia, and thought others like her could be helped. The whole crowd was deeply touched. When the auctioning began, the people responded to the little girl's generosity and spirit. The bidding didn't stop until her lamb sold for $3,000.

I walked away that day heartened by their compassion—*Nina Hermann in* Cheer.

———————

He who says he knows all the answers most likely misunderstood the questions.

The elevator operator has his ups and downs, but he's one of the few who knows where he's going.

Pokes at Cowpokes

Cowboys

Defined: Ranch employee; cowpoke; cowpuncher; wrangler; buckeroo; herdsman; gaucho.

———

Three vacationers of different professions happened to meet at the Grand Canyon.

They gazed out at the vast chasm in silence and then began to speak.

The clergyman: What an awesome miracle of God!

The scientist: What a magnificent wonder of nature!

The cowboy: What an incredible place to lose a cow!

———

One Texas cowboy is so rich, he has well-to-well carpeting on his range.

During his time as a rancher, Theodore Roosevelt, 26th president of the United States, and one of his cowpunchers, riding over the range, lassoed a maverick, a two-year-old steer that had never been branded. They lit a fire then and there and prepared the branding irons. The part of the range they were on was claimed by Gregor Lang, one of Roosevelt's neighbors. According to the rule among cattlemen the steer therefore belonged to Lang, having been found on his land. As the cowboy applied the brand, Roosevelt said, "Wait, it should be Lang's brand, a thistle."

"That's all right, boss," said the cowboy continuing to apply the brand.

"But you're putting on my brand."

"That's right," said the man, "I always put on the boss's brand."

"Drop that iron," said Roosevelt, "and get back to the ranch and get out. I don't need you anymore."

The cowboy protested, but Roosevelt was adamant. "A man who will steal *for* me will steal *from* me," he declared. So the cowboy went, and the story spread all over the Badlands.

If lawyers are debarred and clergymen defrocked, doesn't it follow that electricians can be delighted; musicians denoted; models deposed; tree surgeons debarked; dry cleaners depressed; and cowboys deranged?—*Virginia Ostman.*

The door swung open. A cowboy rushed out, took a running jump, and landed in the gutter.

"What's the matter with you, Fella?" asked a bystander. "Did they kick you out, or are you just plain loco?"

"Neither," said the cowboy, "but I sure would like to lay my hands on the critter who moved my horse!"

———

Cowboys who rub down ponies have reoccurring throat problems. They're always feeling a little hoarse.

———

And then there was the cowboy who only bought one spur. He figured if one side of the horse went, the other would too.

———

I'm an old cowhand, from the Rio Grande,
And my legs ain't bowed, and my skin ain't tanned.
I'm a cowboy who never saw a cow,
Never roped a steer 'cause I don't know how,
And I ain't a-fixin' to start in now,
Yippee-ai-oh-ky-ay.

—*Folk song*

A Texas cowboy doesn't brand his cattle, he engraves them.

———————

When one Texas cowboy was prospecting for oil, all the others sent him get-well cards.

Cow Towns

A cow town is one where there is no place to go where you shouldn't be.

———————

The folks in one Texas cow town used to resist progress, but not anymore. "We're getting a new Studebaker dealership next week."

———————

In a small town the stock market is the place where they sell cattle.

———————

A cow town is a town where you can park as long as you want to, but don't want to.

———————

Nothing makes it easier to resist temptation than living in a small town.

One cow town is so small, the zip code is a fraction.

———————

It's the kind of town where the Sunday paper could be delivered by a carrier pigeon.

———————

Cow town: One where you can chat for a while on the phone even if you get a wrong number.

———————

The barber at the second chair says he comes from a community that's so small there's not enough going on to have a town gossip.

———————

The small town symphony orchestra had to cancel its performance of Beethoven's Fifth. The fellow who played first ukulele quit.

———————

This one cow town was so dull they used to print the newspaper three weeks in advance.

———————

This town was so poor, the fat lady in the circus weighed only 135 pounds.

One Texas town was so poor, it didn't have grain elevators—only grain stairways.

Cow town: One where, if you see a girl dining with a man old enough to be her father, he is.

The town was so small "entering" and "leaving" were on the same sign.

Cow Crazies

Did you hear about the cowhand who's been using a toothbrush on cows' teeth—and now they're giving dental cream?

Tam: Why does your uncle keep his cows in the house?

Sam: Well, he has to keep them contented, doesn't he?

Jane: Did you ever live on a farm and listen to the cowbells?

John: Don't be silly. Cows don't have bells—they have horns.

Sal: How's your father coming with his dairy farm?

Cal: Grand! He makes all the cows sleep on their backs.

Sal: What's the idea?

Cal: So the cream will be on the top in the morning.

———

Tim: Name five things for me that contain milk.

Kim: That's easy. Ice cream, butter, cheese, and two cows.

———

Sandy: Is this milk fresh?

Randy: Fresh? Three hours ago it was grass.

———

Bill: I'm going to sue the railroad company on account of my cows.

Till: What happened, did a train run over your cows?

Bill: No. The trains run so slowly the people lean out the windows and milk my cows.

———

To keep milk from turning sour, keep it in the cow.

Ann: Hey, this milk is colored.

Jan: Sure. This is blue-grass country.

———————

Ted: What is cowhide chiefly used for?

Red: To keep the cow together.

———————

Peg: Say, what kind of a cow gives evaporated milk?

Meg: A dry cow.

———————

Bob: Does a cow give milk?

Rob: No, you have to take it from her!

———————

It was so cold the farmer milked for 20 minutes before he found out he was only shaking hands with himself.

———————

Kim: Do you know how long cows should be milked?

Jim: The same as short cows.

It's easy to milk a cow—any jerk can do it!

———————

His farm is so small that cows only give condensed milk.

———————

Walter: Say, waiter, this milk is weak.

Waiter: Sorry, the cow got caught in the rain.

———————

Life is rough on the farm: You go to sleep with the chickens, get up with the roosters, work like a horse, eat like a pig, and then are treated like a dog

———————

Milkmaid to cow at milking time: Look out, the yanks are coming!

———————

A future dairy farmer is an overall person.

———————

In dairy farming, it takes pull to get ahead.

———————

You might describe a cow that has just given birth to an offspring as de-calf-inated!

Now we know why the cow jumped over the moon—the farmer had cold hands.

While a farm girl was milking a cow, a bull tore across the meadow toward her. The girl did not stir, but continued milking. Observers, who had run to safety, saw to their amazement that the bull stopped dead within a few yards of the girl, turned round and walked sadly away. "Weren't you afraid?" asked everyone.

"Certainly not," said the girl. "I happened to know this cow is his mother-in-law."

A farmer was the owner of a prize Jersey heifer. A stranger, having admired the animal browsing on the hillside, drove around the hill to the farmer's home, and asked:

"How much will you take for your cow?"

The farmer scratched his head for a moment, and then said: "Look-a-here, be you the tax-assessor, or has she been killed by the railroad?"

It was so hot on the range the cows were giving evaporated milk.

Little Johnny, a city boy in the country for the first time, saw the milking of a cow.

"Now you know where the milk comes from, don't you?" he was asked.

"Sure!" replied Johnny. "You give the cow some breakfast food and water and then drain the crankcase."

———————

A lady complained to her milkman of the quality of milk he sold her.

"Well, mum," said the milkman, "the cows don't get enough grass feed this time o' year. Why them cows are just as sorry about it as I am. I often see 'em cryin'—regular cryin', mum—because they feel as how their milk don't do 'em credit. Don't you believe it, mum?"

"Oh, yes, I believe it," responded his customer, "but I wish in the future you'd see that they don't drop their tears into our can."

———————

A farmer married a girl from a town, and found on the return from the honeymoon that she had not the slightest idea of farm work. So he took her out to the barn to break her in at milking the cows.

But the big animals scared her, and she said:

"I don't think I'll be able to milk those big cows, Josh. Couldn't we just start with one of the calves?"

The farmer was driving down a country road and as he slowed to make a turn, another car approached. It was being driven by a rather large woman who yelled out her open window one word, "Pig!"

Not to be outdone, the surprised farmer shouted in return, "Cow!" To his consternation, as he rounded the bend, there right in front of him was an enormous pig.

In the small Idaho community where I used to live, many residents are farmers. Because of emergencies that often arise—sick animals, muddy roads, malfunctioning machinery—people are rarely on time for events.

When the new pastor at the church realized this, he posted the following notice for worship services:

OLA COMMUNITY CHURCH

SUNDAY SCHOOL .... 10 ish
WORSHIP SERVICE .... 11 ish

—*Wilma J. Cole*

If the bravest are the tenderest, the cow that provided our dinner was a coward.

Even if you're on the right track, you'll get run over if you just sit there.

Hey, diddle diddle,
The cat and the fiddle;
The cow jumped over the moon.
So now you know
Why milk's scarce and high—
Please, Bossy, come down soon!

Old bankers never die, they just lose interest.

Old golfers never die, they just putter away.

Old volcanoes never die, they just blow their tops.

Old quarterbacks never die, they just pass away.

Old cows never die, they just kick the bucket.

Old teachers never die, they just lose their class.

Old principals never die, they just lose their faculties.

Old accountants never die, they just lose their balance.

Old farmers never die, they just go to seed.

Old scuba divers never die, they just get their depth certificates.

Jill: What are you going to eat?

Jack: Calves' brains and oxtail soup.

Jill: That's one way of making ends meet.

Teacher: Henry, analyze the sentence, "It was getting to be milking time." What mood?

Henry: The cow.

———————

Tom: What makes this milk so blue?

Tim: It comes from discontented cows.

———————

"During the war, my brother stayed home and worked on the farm. One day while he was milking a cow, a soldier came along and said, 'You slacker! Why aren't you at the front?'"

"What did your brother say?"

"He said, 'Because there isn't any milk at that end.'"

———————

Cal: That cowboy broke his neck at the rodeo.

Jan: How did he break it?

Cal: They gave him a bum steer.

———————

Missus: Don't bring any of that milk. It's positively blue.

Farmer: It ain't our fault, lady. It's these long dull evenings that make the cows depressed.

"It's true, the train killed your cow," admitted the railroad's insurance adjuster to the farmer, "but your cow had no right being on the track.

"She was trespassing and so, in a sense, you were trespassing. Now the railroad is sorry about the loss of your cow, but railroads are run for a profit and they can't afford to go to court for every petty case like this. Tell me, what would you consider a fair settlement?"

"Well, I'm a poor man," replied the farmer, "but I guess I could give you $5."

———

You can tell when you're on the right track—it's all uphill.

———

All tracks to the station of success and achievement are uphill.

Lazy Butchers are Meat Loafers

I'm so naive. Up until I met this butcher, I never knew Rolls-Royce made a delivery truck.

———

My butcher has a very interesting scale. Yesterday a fly landed on it—4½ pounds!

It's incredible! The butchers claim they're not making any money. The wholesalers claim they're not making any money. The ranchers claim they're not making any money. So who's making the money? Sometimes I get the uneasy feeling there are cows buying mutual funds!

Beef prices are so high, I'm on a very special kind of diet. I go to the butcher shop and eat my heart out!

You know you're in trouble when the butcher puts the wax paper on the scale and that alone weighs 38 cents!

The saddest story I ever heard was about a butcher who wanted to become a brain surgeon—but he couldn't afford the cut in pay.

One New York newspaper ran a clever headline on meat prices and inflation: Prices soar, buyers sore, cows jump over the moon.

Out of the Bullpen

A holy cow is entitled to a divorce—if she gets a bum steer.

Political speeches are like the horns on a steer—a point here and a point there with a lot of bull in between.

———

Show me a man who sleeps during a political speech and I'll show you a bulldozer.

———

While my husband was teaching at a small state agricultural college, a proposal to raise faculty salaries was brought before the legislature. The farm bloc was solidly against the measure—they couldn't see why the state should pay those college professors $5000 a year just for talking 12 or 15 hours a week. Faculty representatives made no headway with their arguments until one of them, who had done some farming, had an inspiration.

"Gentlemen," he said to the lawmakers, "a college professor is a little like a bull. It's not the amount of time he spends. It's the importance of what he does!"

The professors got their raise.

———

Expecting the world to treat you fairly because you are a good person is a little like expecting the bull not to attack you because you're a vegetarian.

The bull bellows loudest;
    The cow gives the milk.
A butterfly is beautiful;
    The worm spins the silk.
And barreled goods are valued
    By the contents (not the keg).
The rooster does the crowing,
    It's the hen that lays the egg.

He was like a bull in a china shop until she cowed him.

Did you know that John Small, who saved his life by playing his violin to a ferocious bull, to "the admiration and perfect satisfaction of the mischievous beast," lived to be 89? (Small was a famous 18th-century cricketer.)

When you take a bull by the horns...what happens is a toss-up—*W. Pett Ridge*.

Hitching Your Wagon to a Star

Two cows watched the milk truck drive by with this sign painted on it: Pure milk—Pasteurized—Homogenized—Vitamin D Added!

One cow commented to the other: Makes you feel a bit inadequate, doesn't it?

What's it going to take to make you feel adequate to face life's demands?

Advice

The way to be successful is to follow the advice you give to others.

Good advice is no better than poor advice, unless you follow it.

It's a pleasure to give advice, humiliating to need it, and normal to ignore it.

———————

Advice is least heeded when most needed.

———————

"Be yourself" is about the worst advice you can give to some people.

Determination

Most men fail, not through lack of education, but from lack of dogged determination, from lack of dauntless will.

———————

Getting wisdom is the most important thing you can do! And with your wisdom, develop common sense and good judgment (Proverbs 4:7).

———————

Today's mighty oak is just yesterday's nut that held its ground.

———————

A diamond is a chunk of coal that stuck to its job.

People may doubt what you say, but they'll always believe what you do.

———

Giving it another try is better than an alibi.

———

Thinking well is wise; planning well, wiser; doing well is wisest of all.

———

Even if you're on the right track, you'll get run over if you just sit there—*Will Rogers*.

———

Many people have the right aim in life, but they never pull the trigger.

———

Those who act receive the prizes—*Aristotle*.

———

Whatsoever thy hand findeth to do, do it with thy might (Ecclesiastes 9:10 KJV).

———

He started to sing as he tackled the thing that couldn't be done, and he did it—*Edgar Guest*.

Chin and Win

Square your shoulders to the world!
   It's easy to give in,
Lift your chin a little higher!
   You were made to win.

Grit your teeth, but smile, don't frown,
   We all must bear our bit.
It's not the load that weighs us down,
   It's the way we carry it.

———

In golf and in life, it's the follow-through that makes the difference.

———

No man in the world has more determination than he who can stop after eating one peanut.

Decision

Almost everyone knows the difference between right and wrong, but some just hate to make decisions.

———

At the crossroads in a southwestern desert state was this sign: Be careful which road you decide to take—you'll be on it for the next 200 miles!

More people fail through lack of purpose than lack of talent—*Billy Sunday.*

Never make a decision based on fear.

Goals: Write them down; hang them up; pray them through; and with God's help, watch them happen!

Long-range goals keep you from being frustrated by short-term failures.

So I run straight to the goal with purpose in every step. I fight to win. I'm not just shadow-boxing or playing around (1 Corinthians 9:26).

Choice, not chance, determines destiny.

You can't make a place for yourself under the sun if you keep sitting in the shade of the family tree.

Some men dream of worthy accomplishments, while others stay awake and do them.

Dream and Scheme

The agriculture-school dean was interviewing a freshman. "Why have you chosen this career?" he asked.

"I dream of making a million dollars in farming like my father," replied the freshman.

The dean was impressed. "Your father made a million dollars in farming?"

"No," replied the student, "but he always dreamed of it!"

———

It doesn't do any harm to dream as long as you get up and hustle when the alarm goes off.

———

People who are always walking on clouds leave too many things up in the air.

———

Success is the ability to hitch your wagon to a star while keeping your feet on the ground.

Do not love sleep or you will grow poor; stay awake and you will have food to spare (Proverbs 20:13 NIV).

Investigation

A person who asks questions may be a fool for five minutes; he who never asks a question remains a fool forever.

———

Don't be afraid to ask dumb questions. They're easier to handle than dumb mistakes.

———

What a shame—yes, how stupid!—to decide before knowing the facts! (Proverbs 18:13).

———

Four and 17 are the most desirable ages; at four, you know all the questions; at 17, you know all the answers.

———

People who jump to conclusions usually make a bad landing.

Listening

No man ever listened himself out of a job— *Calvin Coolidge*.

Don't talk so much. You keep putting your foot in your mouth. Be sensible and turn off the flow! When a good man speaks he is worth listening to, but the words of fools are a dime a dozen (Proverbs 10:19,20).

———

Did you hear about the husband who called his wife to the phone: Dear, somebody wants to listen to you!

Satisfaction

Here are five keys to fulfillment: Obey your great Creator; dream great dreams; plan great plans; pray great prayers; and claim great victories.

———

Nature gave me two ends—one to sit on and the other to think with. Man's success or failure depends on which one he uses most.

———

He who delays struggles with failure and lack of fulfillment.

———

He who chooses a job he likes will never have to work a day of his life.

Be the Best of Whatever You Are

If you can't be a pine on the top of the
    hill,
  Be a scrub in the valley—but be
The best little scrub by the side of the
    rill;
  Be a bush if you can't be a tree.

If you can't be a bush, be a bit of the grass,
  Some highway happier make;
If you can't be a muskie, then just be a
    bass—
  But the liveliest bass in the lake!

We can't all be captains, we've got to be
    crew,
  There's something for all of us here,
There's big work to do, and there's lesser
    to do,
  And the task we must do is the near.

If you can't be a highway, then just be a trail,
  If you can't be the sun, be a star;
It isn't by size that you win or you fail—
  Be the best of whatever you are!
            —*Douglas Malloch*

Other Good Harvest House Reading

LOVE LINES
by *Vern McLellan*

In *Love Lines* you will find the perfect expression of love and laughter. Whether it's just for fun or to fan the fire of romance, Vern McLellan presents quotes and amazing anecdotes that get to the heart of the matter!

WISE WORDS FROM A WISE GUY
by *Vern McLellan*

Back with his latest collection of the wise and wacky, master wordsmith Vern McLellan is ready to brighten your life and conversation with illustrated principles and humor based on the sayings of Solomon and others.

Filled with a multitude of conversation-starters, quick comebacks, and inspirational morsels delightfully illustrated by Sandy Silverthorne, *Wise Words from a Wise Guy* is a perfect gift—for yourself or a friend—with a wisdom-filled message!

SHREDDED WIT
by *Vern McLellan*

Crisp, crackling, popping-good one liners from the author of *Proverbs for People* and *Quips, Quotes, and Quests*. A "bran" new serving of insightful bitefuls of wit and wisdom. Supplement your diet with hundreds of delightful and inspirational morsels of high fiber humor. Over 100,000 Vern McLellan books now in print!

PROVERBS FOR PEOPLE
by *Vern McLellan*

Clever proverbs are matched with a corresponding Scripture reference and illustration that will bring a smile and a cause for reflection with the turn of each page.

PROVERBS, PROMISES, AND PRINCIPLES
by *Vern McLellan*

A stimulating new collection of thought-provoking sayings and colorful anecdotes to give your life and conversation a lift. Contains hundreds of new topics handled in a skillful and readable style. By the author of *Quips, Quotes, and Quests*.

THE ALL-NEW CLEAN JOKE BOOK
by *Bob Phillips*

Over 850 all-new jokes in this wild and wacky collection. Crazy quotations and humorous advertisements make this a laugh-a-minute book that you won't want to set down.

THE BEST OF THE GOOD CLEAN JOKES
by *Bob Phillips*

Bestselling humorist Bob Phillips compiles the "best of the best" in his newest collection of wholesome humor. Preachers, teachers, family, and friends—anyone who enjoys good clean jokes— won't want to miss this laugh-filled resource from the pen of the master joker. Bob Phillips' 11 joke and fun books have sold more than two million copies.

THE ALL AMERICAN JOKE BOOK
by *Bob Phillips*

A riotous, fun-filled collection of over 800 anecdotes, puns, and jokes.

MORE GOOD CLEAN JOKES
by *Bob Phillips*

An entertaining fun-book designed for public speakers, pastors, and everyone who enjoys good clean jokes.

THE RETURN OF THE GOOD CLEAN JOKES
by *Bob Phillips*
Over 900 quips, anecdotes, gags, puns, and wisecracks.

WIT AND WISDOM
by *Charlie "T" Jones* and *Bob Phillips*

Bestselling humorist Bob Phillips combines his talent with the unforgettable Charlie "Tremendous" Jones and takes you through the alphabet laughing all the way.

THE WORLD'S GREATEST COLLECTION OF DAFFY DEFINITIONS/RIDDLES
by *Bob Phillips*

In this double-dose of laughs, you'll find riddles on topics ranging from time, food, and love to spelling and children *OR* turn the book over and enjoy the latest and greatest collection of crazy "one-liners" yet assembled by the master compiler of wit and humor.

THE LAST OF THE GOOD CLEAN JOKES
by *Bob Phillips*

The master joker edits and arranges wisecracks, rib ticklers, and zany puns.

THE WORLD'S GREATEST COLLECTION OF CLEAN JOKES
by *Bob Phillips*

For everyone who enjoys wholesome humor. This collection of 1000 jokes has already sold over 250,000 copies.

THE WORLD'S GREATEST COLLECTION OF HEAVENLY HUMOR
by *Bob Phillips*

Proof once again that it is not necessary for Christians to go through life with a sour disposition. A masterful collection of heavenly jokes.

Dear Reader:

We would appreciate hearing from you regarding this Harvest House nonfiction book. It will enable us to continue to give you the best in Christian publishing.

1. What most influenced you to purchase *Cream of Wit*?
   - [ ] Author
   - [ ] Subject matter
   - [ ] Backcover copy
   - [ ] Recommendations
   - [ ] Cover/Title
   - [ ] _____

2. Where did you purchase this book?
   - [ ] Christian bookstore
   - [ ] General bookstore
   - [ ] Other
   - [ ] Grocery store
   - [ ] Department store

3. Your overall rating of this book:
   - [ ] Excellent
   - [ ] Very good
   - [ ] Good
   - [ ] Fair
   - [ ] Poor

4. How likely would you be to purchase other books by this author?
   - [ ] Very likely
   - [ ] Somewhat likely
   - [ ] Not very likely
   - [ ] Not at all

5. What types of books most interest you? (check all that apply)
   - [ ] Women's Books
   - [ ] Marriage Books
   - [ ] Current Issues
   - [ ] Self Help/Psychology
   - [ ] Bible Studies
   - [ ] Fiction
   - [ ] Biographies
   - [ ] Children's Books
   - [ ] Youth Books
   - [ ] Other _____

6. Please check the box next to your age group.
   - [ ] Under 18
   - [ ] 18-24
   - [ ] 25-34
   - [ ] 35-44
   - [ ] 45-54
   - [ ] 55 and over

Mail to: Editorial Director
Harvest House Publishers
1075 Arrowsmith
Eugene, OR 97402

Name _____

Address _____

City _____ State _____ Zip _____